HOW TO
HIGH SCHOOL

22 Simple Insights to Support Your Journey

J.D. DURDEN

J.D. Durden
For permission requests, contact howtohighschool@jddurden.com

Printed Worldwide
First Printing 2023
First Edition 2023

Book Design by Krystal Penney
Cover Artwork by JSCD
Cover Photography & Cube by LTCD
For more information about booking and bulk purchases, please connect at
www.jddurden.com

Disclaimer
The information contained in this book is intended for educational coaching only. The content in this book is not for diagnosis, prescription, or treatment of any disorder, and should not replace consultation with healthcare professionals.

If you or someone you know needs help, please seek an adult you can trust, call 911 or call 988 for Suicide and Crisis Lifeline (Available 24 hours).

Be purposeful in your practice.
Be mindful in your choices.
Be brave in your action.
Be all you were born To Be.

-J.D. Durden
(aka Mrs. D. & Mom)

DEDICATION

For my daughter and son. You have inspired me to be a better human. You both motivate me to make education better, for not only you, but for all youth. My greatest role in life is to be your mama, to watch you grow, and support you while you continue your journey. You are my True Sky.

To my fourteen nieces and five nephews. Whether you are out of high school, or just starting on your school journey, thank you for teaching me so much. Being an aunt is one of my favorite jobs ever. Not only did you make me a better mom, but you have taught me so much about your own experience and stages of life so I could write this book with even more confidence.

ACKNOWLEDGEMENTS

To all students who have crossed my path via classrooms, social-emotional workshops, clubs, sports, and surveys. If not for you, I would not live such an enriched journey of knowledge for how our youth walk through this life. If not for you, I wouldn't be inspired to collect this knowledge and write it down for our future generations. If not for you, I wouldn't still be learning.

TABLE OF CONTENTS

PREFACE

I'm not a doctor.
I'm not a therapist.
I'm a teacher
who listens to the students in front of me.

In my career, my focus has been on creating spaces where youth feel safe, seen, and supported. This book is no different. I desperately want this world to be better for our youth who are going into it. I sincerely believe that each individual human experience contributes to the greater experience in our homes, schools, communities, and world.

How to High School was inspired through one consistent question I have always asked senior classes I've taught: "What do you wish you would have known before you graduated high school?" This question is the foundation of this book. Over the past twenty years, so much has changed for our youth. For past generations to compare our experiences to today's youth is like comparing gas prices from then to now. Social media, college requirements, lack of safety in schools, and more, has shaped our youth's experience, but the topics within this book remain consistent no matter the changes in the greater world.

I have released this book at the same time as my daughter is heading into high school and my son enters sixth grade. I've been writing this book in my head for the last twenty years of teaching. It's no accident that now would be the time that my observations and human data collecting would fall out of my heart and into this book.

My hope is that *How to High School* gives insight to high school students all over the world and provides a safe place to find realistic answers as you move through **your journey**.

Thank you for being here with me.

1

THIS WORLD IS YOURS

I know this world seems so big

And everything seems so out of reach

The sky is high and the walk is wide

You just don't know what you got yet

It's in the palm of your hands

It's right in front of where you stand

If you believe, everything you dream will come true

If you can love no matter how you hurt,

Love will come to you, back to you

This world is yours

At times I know it's going to be hard

When you think you can't go on

But there's a plan for you just let your heart follow through

Come on, I promise you can do it all

Cause where you fall you can always start again

Your future's right in front of where you stand

If you believe, everything you dream will come true

If you can love no matter how you hurt,

Love will come to you, back to you

This world is yours

Climb a mountain

Cross the ocean

Sail the river until it opens

Make good friends, listen hard

Let it out, and dance on

If you believe, everything you dream will come true

If you can see there's nothing that can be too big for you

If you can see, if you can believe, if you can dream

This world is yours.

© J.D Durden

Dear Inspiring Youth,

I wrote this song on the very first day my daughter entered preschool as a two-year-old. We were a little nervous dropping her off. She was giddy, talkative, and ready to start her next journey. She is a warrior. She was born to do life to the fullest. After leaving her at the preschool in someone else's care, I drove home, walked into a quiet house, went into my studio, and picked up my guitar. This song poured out and was written in no time at all. While writing, I cried tears of joy and pride processing her possible journey. This song showed up as my dedication to her future.

When this song was released into the world, it became one of the most played graduation songs in the world and still is to this day. Yes, the world. What a surprise to me as this song took on a life of its own for graduations of all levels. It also made sense, because my world is dedicated to being a mom, teaching and songwriting. It was also clear to me that my path forward would merge all three. Welcome to my worlds as I continue to remind you that 'this world is yours'.

"Teaching is my passion. Songwriting is my soul. Love is my journey."– J.D. Durden

2

CHALLENGING BUT DOABLE

I know you are a little worried. Maybe even scared to enter into high school. Some of you are excited to move forward, but still nervous. Your comfort zones are being tested, and that is *uncomfortable* to say the least. It doesn't matter where you are on the fear scale; the truth is, you are ready. You have what it takes to enter into the unknown and slowly gain your confidence. While you are gaining your confidence, I'd like to give you three simple affirmations you can keep saying to yourself until you feel more comfortable.

Keep breathing deeply.

This will get easier.

I am here because I matter.

If you are wondering if high school will be challenging, please accept that it will be—for the most part. Whether you want to be the top of your class or simply move through high school to get to your next stage of life, on all levels, you can certainly expect a challenge.

It's not only the uptick of schoolwork and homework. It is also the managing of your life around school. As the work increases to prepare you for the afterworld of high school, many of you will also play sports, work, take care of your family, and try to care for yourself. Your adolescent stage right now wants independence, but also, you are a little uncomfortable in being entirely solo. Your adolescent development, chemical and hormonal changes, along with navigating all that life has to offer can be overwhelming to say the least. You have distractions all around you from friendships to social media, and you still have to somehow remain focused long enough to be successful in each step that you take on this journey. Later in this book, I will be focusing on the mistakes we all make and that it's ok to make mistakes as long as we can get back on track and move forward. But for now, you have to ask yourself … "Am I ready for this challenge or not?"

The truth is, whether you are ready or not, it's happening! Just like the years before when you were not sure about change in a new grade, with new teachers, new friends, new classrooms—you still did it! You were successful in navigating the past unknowns. Congratulations!

Now, you will be successful again in this new journey called *high school.*

Dear Worried Youth,

I dare you to try to find some sort of joy and excitement in this new adventure. Only you can shift your mindset to the place of accepting this really important challenge. Be in the moment and embrace your experiences. Your time in high school will be short … don't rush things.

I believe in you and you are capable of achieving whatever you want.

You got this,

Mrs. D.

3

PRACTICE FAILURE

"Practicing failure" sounds like nails on a chalkboard to many of us. Why would anyone in their right mind want to practice failing? Doesn't it come naturally and painfully enough already? Yes, it does feel like we fail enough. Yes, it does feel like we fail much more than we succeed. Your feeling is not wrong. Validating failure in this crazy game of life, is quite important to winning in the game of life. "Important to what?" you ask. Success. Failure is the most important ingredient for true success and personal growth. I know, we have certainly coined the term "failure" as the worst thing that could happen in our world, but stick with me here. We are going to reshape what this word means and if we should even use the term at all in our communications. Merriam-Webster defines the word "failure" as: "a falling short or lack of success."[1]

Ok, first and foremost, we have been using the term "failure" as a verb that can really mess up our psyche. But, in reality, failing is simply falling short of something you have tried. I say, kudos to you for even trying! Secondly, ask any adult, failure does not mean lack of success *unless* we allow it to keep us from growing and trying new things over and over. The only time we can use the word "fail" literally is for a test of some sort, "Oh, man, I failed that test." Still, I argue that you are learning how to fail less and still learned information and lessons for next time.

When my daughter started experiencing what she felt were failures, she went from an "All-in, I got this, I love new things, move out of my way" type of personality, to rarely trying new things because she didn't like the feeling of failing. This is natural and certainly a culprit of where anxieties start developing. No matter how many times I would say, "Just go for it, you have nothing to lose," she felt differently inside. The perspective I was speaking from was that of an adult who had lived through dump-trucks full of failure and realized that they didn't break me. An adult with a lot of tools in my toolbox for dealing with life. For her, as a pre-teen and teen, the possibility of failing showed up as anxiety which made her hesitant to try new things, even though she might have wanted to deep down. She's working through all of this, and my guess is, so are you. I have witnessed hundreds of teens at your age go through these times where anxieties create insecurities. But, what if we replaced the term "fail-ure" with "failvent-ure"? Now, "failventure" is not in the dictionary as one word, I came up with it while thinking about the adventures we are on when we feel we have failed. Shifting the noun "failure" into a space where it can bring a positive experience. Every single human on this planet is on an amazing adventure that's naturally going to be full of failing *opportunities.* According to Durden's Dictionary, "Failvent-ure" means: "finding adventure within the opportunities life gives us to fail."

There's a song that I dedicate to my own kids and my students. It's called "I Wish You Pain" by Andy Grammer. I know … that sounds like a dreadful song title to dedicate, but ask yourself this: where would you be without experiencing pain and failure? If I was a mom or teacher who protected those whom I love so much that they were saved from pain, hurt, or failure, then I would be holding them back from learning lessons, maturing in new ways, and growing. Pain is part of failure and failure is part of pain … and they both direct your path on an amazing adventure. The song lyrics go like this:

Cause I love you more than you could know
And your heart, it grows every time it breaks
I know that it might sound strange
But I wish you pain
Wish you pain
It's hard to say
But I wish you pain

"It's hard to say, but I wish you pain" is how we grow and one of the ways we can move into new stages of life. For example, say you love the sport of basketball, and you want to see how good you are, but you are too scared to fail, so you don't try out for the school team. *Will others be better than me? Am I good enough?* First, if you don't try out, you will never know the answer to any of these questions. Second, the answer to these questions does not matter if you love the game. Third, if you don't *try*, that's the true definition of *failing.* We develop our own protective behavioral mechanisms that talk us out of trying new things. This is called behavioral programming. You are a better you for *trying* no matter the outcome.

Behavioral programming starts happening with if-then statements that we say to ourselves. This example of if-then statements lead to lack of success and there's no way around it.

If I don't *try*, then I can't *fail.*

If I don't *fail,* then I *can't* feel bad.

If I don't feel bad, then life is easier …

Here's a more positive form of behavioral programming for a different outcome.

If I do *try*, then I might *fail.*

If I don't *try,* then I will never know.

If I never know, then … well … I will never know!

Sometimes the never knowing can be a haunting feeling of failure all on its own.

Let's try again.

If I do *try,* then I might *fail.*

If I don't *try,* then I will never know.

If I never know, then I might miss my opportunity to be successful and fulfill my dreams.

I need to take a step into adventure, no matter the outcome.

Rationalizing and conditioning in this way is typical for all humans. It's a common practice in health psychology. The problem is, by the time we rationalize to the point of "then life is easier," we've just made a behavioral decision to escape the possibility of pain, disappointment, and failure. We miss the adventure. Momentarily, that might feel good or relieving. But you have now missed possible opportunities to grow, to reflect, to know yourself better, and to experience success. The reality of taking the "life is easier" road, is that it doesn't feel good. Letting ourselves down is worse than letting anyone else down. But what *if* you try, *then* things turn out better than you ever dreamed?

So, in order to experience "failvent-ure," the only option is to try. There are far more noes in life than there are yeses. There are far more failures than successes. But I promise you we remember the successes far more than the failures. We grow more with multiple fails than with one success. Our paths in life are literally steered by our failures that lead to successes. In my life, this is a quote I made up and it gives me peace each time I'm told no: "The word *no* is our life compass that leads to the right *yes*."

Practicing failure means you are allowing yourself to experience pain. Practicing failure means that you are bracing yourself, taking care of yourself, holding boundaries, and preparing for possible failure, with the hope and possibility of success.

Enjoy your failvent-ures.

Trust the process.

Be brave.

Try.

Dear Brilliant Youth,

Disclaimer: There are important times in life when the "if-then" scenario works in our favor when we are in bad, toxic, or unhealthy situations/relationships. This is different than what I am writing about in this chapter on practicing failure. When we need to get out of a negative or bad situation, getting to the "life is easier" without this "thing or person" is a very important decision and can be a huge success in life.

You are an incredible human who deals with human stuff. This does not devalue you. You are deserving of the very best life possible, so go for it.

You got this,

Mrs. D.

4

THE ENOUGH-NESS MONSTER

In my quest over the years of observing and trying to understand high school youth, there is one major theme that rises to the surface more often than anything else. Enough-ness.

Am I "enough?"

I do not feel like I'm "enough."

I don't know how to be "enough."

Enough already!

I may or may not know you personally, but I do know you. Year after year of working with high school teens and asking the same social-emotional questions over and over, I always get the same answers. You can definitely be 100% sure that whatever you are feeling right now in your life, you are not alone! In fact, more than one billion adolescents in the world feel like you do. It does not matter your country, economic status, race, religion, or gender; humans your age physiologically and psychologically go through similar experiences. During this stage, you experience many changes and there are a lot of unknowns. "The Enough-ness Monster" is living secretly inside humans of all ages, so let's talk through how to take this monster down early in life.

I could tell you all day long, just like I do my own children, "You are enough—more than enough—I promise." But that doesn't change how you feel about yourself. Chances are, if you are reading this book, you are in middle adolescence (13–18 years of age) or late adolescence (19–21 years of age). There are so many physiological changes that are occurring with your body and mind. Life gets overly emotional and the awkwardness hits new levels. But at the same time, there are cognitive changes occurring that give you greater capacity to think more broadly and critically about morals and the meaning of life. Most of the time you don't realize or understand that these changes are going on, and you simply think you can't handle life—which leads to questioning everything. Again, this is natural. You are still changing and developing as a human while at the same time the world gives you high expectations to handle. Whew! I get exhausted thinking about this part of life for you (and honestly wouldn't go back there)! All generations before you are proof that it all does get better.

Along with your physical and cognitive development that continues during these stages, your social-emotional development is in need of support. As much as you want to be independent, you still need some help emotionally and this is ok. Here are some of the social-emotional topics that you carry around with you each day:

- You want more independence.
- Popularity starts to mean more than it should.
- You start to get paranoid about what others think.
- You get crushes and have heartbreaks.

- You develop new interests and dreams for your life.
- Friendships make or break everything.
- Social media influence.
- Peer pressure.
- Demands and expectations in school.
- Worrying about your future.
- Fear of failure and fear of not being "normal" . . . wait! Who decides what's normal?

It's no wonder that you feel like you are not good enough. This is a lot to manage all at once. The truth is, as you mature and move into adulthood, you will develop more tools to handle all of this well. Hang in there. For now, let's talk about what you can do to keep moving along your journey and continue defeating The Enough-ness Monster." What a threat to all humankind!

First, let's try to understand what created this Enough-ness Monster. Simply explained, the monster is your insecurities. Merriam-Webster dictionary describes "insecurity" as: "a state or feeling of anxiety, fear, or self-doubt."[2] That self-doubt has single-handedly created this Enough-ness Monster within you. Many factors these days create that self-doubt. For example, the longer we watch all of the perfected social media reels or shorts, the more vulnerable we are to allow the monster to take over. But, we have to be aware enough to block this monster when it shows up. It doesn't happen overnight, but you can shut it down.

Here are some ways to get into a new mindset and take down the Enough-ness Monster little by little:

- The Enough-ness Monster is repelled by positivity, self-love, and anyone who wants to change their life for the better.

- Please take it upon yourself to realize the moments that make you feel self-doubt and insecurity. Reflect on why you are feeling these feelings. Is it because of the people around you? Is it because you are trying something new? Is it because you feel judged? Are you judging yourself too harshly?

- Take a break from social media. Stay off for as long you need. Rest your eyes, your brain, and your competition with others. Be free from social media in order to reset your brain patterns. You well know the addiction to this part of your life, and how social media can make any human feel they are not "good enough." There are far too many comparisons and false perfections to keep up with on social media. The amount of time we spend getting stuck scrolling is enough to make us upset with ourselves. This is an easy fix. Put your phone in another room and set time boundaries for yourself.

- Write yourself positive thoughts on your mirror each day. Look at yourself in that mirror and say, "I am enough." So what if it feels weird? You have a monster to get rid of!

- Don't use the word "normal." Change to "typical" or "natural." Who decides what's normal anyway?

- If someone else makes you feel bad about yourself, evaluate the relationship and make changes. If it's an adult, let them know—if it's safe to do so. If it's a friend, ask yourself why you are in this relationship. You are strong enough to make important mental-health changes for yourself in this way.

- Listen to the people who are consistently lifting you up. They are not just saying nice things. What they are saying is true! Don't let the monster make you doubt them.

- Find a positive and safe role model like a teacher, coach, or family member you can trust who you can go to in times of doubt or need.

- Understand that you are not supposed to have all of the answers right now—not even half of the answers.

- You don't need to have your entire life planned out right now. You have time and everyone takes a different route.

- Do what you love. It's not about anyone else.

- Do what will make you feel good inside and makes you genuinely smile. It's not about what someone else does or doesn't do.

- Do what will spark your unique spirit and don't let anyone crush your spirit.

- Keep an honesty journal. Tell your truth. Be honest with yourself—always.
- Exercise. Walk if you don't like to exercise.
- Embrace your differences from others. There's only one of you and one of everyone else.
- Learn to love yourself more and more every single day. It is not selfish to love yourself. No one will take care of you like you do. Self-care is the best way to love yourself.
- Talk your brain into turning negative situations into positive.

Dear Fearless Youth,

Thank you for going there with me in taking down The Enough-ness Monster. With self-love and positivity, no monster can exist within you.

Let me ask you again …

Who decides what's normal?

You do! It's your life!

You got this,

Mrs. D.

5

COMFORT ZONE PARALYSIS

Humans love to stay within our comfort zones, because, well ... it's the most *comforting* place to us (we think). We don't want to stretch outside of our comfort zones because it can cause pain and unwanted anxiety. So, typically, we stay where we are. We don't make any moves because we naturally protect ourselves from that pain or anxiety. I call this space that we don't move out of, "comfort zone paralysis."

Don't get me wrong, comfort zones serve their purpose for us and protect us many times in life. But let's also be clear—there is no growth available to us if we stay within the constraints of our comfort zones. I am not suggesting that you jump out of your zone in every area and jolt your nervous system into panic mode, but I am saying that when you feel you can trust yourself, take some steps outside of the zone. It's important for your future. I have a theory about comfort zones: "your dreams will never meet you in your comfort zone, rather, they wait for you outside of it." So, I dare you to step outside, see what's out there for yourself.

Through behavioral psychology research, the discussion of comfort zones can be traced back to 1907 when Yerkes and Dodson performed motivational experiments on rats.[3] They tested the rats' performance levels and recorded their reactions in order to gauge their anxiety levels. After many more studies done by multiple scientists and psychologists, research led to a progression of our behavioral zones for better understanding.

Comfort Zone → Fear Zone → Learning Zone → Growth Zone

Each of us are in this zone progression at any time of any day. Sometimes multiple times a day. We can move in and out of each zone or hang out in certain zones for a while. We can also have one foot in one zone, while transitioning to the next zone. This zone progression makes perfect sense. What zone(s) are you in right now?

If you think back on any decisions you've had to make, you will find that this is the progression you went through. No matter how old we get, this is our zoning process. We start in our comfort zones, go into our fear zones, and progress from there, or we retreat back into our comfort zones. Most of you reading this book are moving into a new school experience with many areas of possible growth. In order to start feeling comfortable in your new life, you must take steps out of your comfort zone—feeling the fear, learning new things, and growing. How exciting!

As a hyper-aware teacher, I started noticing high school students' behaviors surrounding this topic and realized that many students were stuck in their comfort zone. There was no stepping forward to see what was possible. So, I started calling this behavior, "comfort zone paralysis" and started teaching comfort zone paralysis lessons with students so they could self-evaluate where they were in the zones and possibly transition themselves out of this paralysis.

In my lessons, I ask students to visualize a shape or picture of what their comfort zone process looks like for them. I have them draw it out and label the zones accordingly. For me, my comfort zone resembles a standard Rubik's cube. My son always has Rubik's Cubes lying around the house, and he asked me to try to solve it one day and … voilà! I had my comfort zone reference. A Rubik's cube is made up of twenty-six cubies that make up the bigger cube. There are many layers to this cube when you really think about it. At the core of the cube, when you take the cubies off, there is a deep centered comfort zone or safe zone, and as the layers move outwards, the cubies become the moving parts of your life to represent your fear, learning, and growth. One movement of the outer cubies can shift energy enough to get us safely out of our comfort zone and into learning and growth areas. There's no wrong move when figuring out the steps to solving this puzzle. But making moves and shifts are a necessary function to solving anything.

Facing your fears and stepping outside your comfort zone can allow you to move more freely. Comfort zone paralysis is a real condition where you can get stuck in the comfort zone and never grow, no matter how much you want to grow and move. This zone can feel suffocating. But one step at a time, one risk at a time, one trip and fall at a time, can move you out of comfort zone paralysis into growth flow. If you want something healthy but fear is holding you back, try taking one step or moving one cube to shift the paralysis. Your life is directed by how you shift and move in any situation. Only you can do it. No one else is going to do it for you, and things don't just magically show up at your doorstep (unless it's Amazon). You will have to work for every single healthy thing you want in your life. Only when you get out of your comfort zone in safe ways does life start shaping for you and working for you, but you have to put the time and energy in first. You have to take that first step which requires moving the cubies to get to your next step.

Remember, the healthy things and dreams you want will *never* meet you in your comfort zone; they meet you outside of it. Every. Single. Time.

Dear Brave Youth,

Working hard to move out of your comfort zone might sound awful right now in your stage of life. As a teen, insecurities take over and you don't want to be seen too much by others. You want to stay small in a sense. But know that whatever you do right now directly impacts your future. I know that's heavy, and it's not meant to scare you but, remember, taking risks to better your life is only for healthy decisions. Unhealthy decisions attached to trying new things will not benefit your life, and it might take you a long time to recover. Mistakes are natural in this process, but focus on the healthy steps. Perfection is not what we are looking for here. Remember, practicing failure leads to understanding life better and helps you move outside of your comfort zone paralysis and into shaping your life.

You got this,

Mrs. D.

6

RED FLAGS ARE YOUR SUPERPOWER

I am positive that other humans have left you hurt, confused, and alone. I am sure that as you move forward in age and grade, you will continue to learn to understand the dynamics of human interaction. Whether the relationship is a friend, boyfriend, girlfriend, or an acquaintance, look out for red flags on whether you want to have them in your life or not.

Humans naturally want connections with other humans. During adolescence, you may feel even more need to have friends—to have a place to belong. Friendships are on the top of the list for adolescent relationships. In fact, psychological research proves that for our entire lives, our behavior, emotions, sense of acceptance, and needs are all wrapped up in *belonging*. That's a pretty big deal if you think about it. We are all wrapped up in this sense of belonging at all stages of life. But, as we get older and our awareness of our own needs matures, this process of *needing to belong* gets easier. For right now—in your teen years—any relationship can be a lot but making informed decisions on who to bring into your life and keep, is really important.

I like to use the *red flag* terminology in class, within discussions, or in my own life where we can pinpoint areas of concern. Once identifying the concern, we can pause, think about it, and then make further conclusions for how we want to proceed. We have natural red flags that show up every single day within us that bring caution. It could be as simple as crossing a road. You press the button for the traffic light to signal you to cross the street, and when the light lets you know that it's safe to walk, your brain says "go," but then we still pause … look both ways … and when we decide to take a step we still look around for any threat. The reason we don't just walk across when the signal tells us to is because we have internal red flags that tell us we need to investigate a little deeper. When these red flags go up, we stop, evaluate, and make our conclusions before we act. This is why activating your red flags when needed is …

YOUR SUPERPOWER!

Within relationships, your Red Flag Superpower works the same. First, let's clarify what "relationships" mean. A relationship can be formed between any two entities. In fact, it doesn't even have to be human relationships—as wild as that sounds. Cambridge Dictionary simplifies the meaning as, "the way in which things are connected or work together."[4] You have a relationship with your phone, your car, your dog, your favorite stuffy (yes, still). You also can be connected to other humans. When it comes to human connection or a material connection, activating your Red Flag Superpower System can save you a lot of time, money, heartache, pain, and stress in life.

The Red Flag Superpower System (RFSS) is a simple system that I created through my own mistakes and lessons in life. I realized we all have this superpower; we just aren't aware of it or know how to use it. When caution arises, this simple system organizes our thoughts and feelings to make more informed decisions.

STOP: *Take a Breather.*

EVALUATE: *Find the Truth.*

CONCLUDE: *Own the Truth.*

ACT: *Proceed or Change.*

Red flags aren't always bad, but rather a cautionary state to evaluate if we will be harmed in the relationship or life event. If I am activating the *Red Flag Superpower System* for the overuse of my phone—which I have a strong relationship with—it may go something like this:

STOP

Take a Breather—Put the phone down for a few hours and out of reach of any impulse to pick it up and look at it.

EVALUATE

Find the Truth—How do I feel when I get stuck on my phone? Why do I need to put it down? How am I benefitting from this amount of use? Is this an addiction? Etc.

CONCLUDE

Own the Truth—It makes me lose time with real life and experiences. It makes me feel insecure watching the shorts. It makes me procrastinate on everything else in life. It makes me anxious, which leads to less happiness.

ACT

Proceed or Change—Put phone away when I get home from school until I've completed responsibilities. Lock it away for a certain number of hours on the weekends. Take back my control. Help my anxiety. Be happier.

Of course, you can use this same system for friendship decisions. Not every person you meet in life is someone you should "keep." Not every human will be your best friend. In choosing these relationships, we have to choose wisely. Some humans are jealous and toxic, and they do not want what is best for us. This is when we activate our superpower and "red flag" their importance in our lives. The most emotionally intelligent response to a relationship not benefitting you is to say "no." Being by yourself for a little while is much healthier than being in a relationship where the other side does not value you, burns with jealousy, or tries to tear you down.

On the other side of this, you need to self-check that you are not a "red flag" for someone else—one of these individuals who interact through jealousy, envy, hate, or greed. If you are the human interacting in a rough manner, then others will red flag you, just like in football when the referee throws a flag for too much rough play.

Believe it or not, while I write this chapter, I still have to activate my Red Flag Superpower. As I have matured, I can spot toxicity a mile away, but still, I make constant decisions to accept a relationship or not. Co-workers can be amongst the toughest terrain to navigate when it comes to relationships. Even some adults cannot handle someone else's talent, skill, or knowledge. They get jealous, talk behind co-workers' backs, downplay good work for others, or even bully. Can you believe this still happens? As an adult, I continue to self-check how I show up for others and myself. The great news for you is that you have all of this time to practice the *Red Flag Superpower System* (RFSS) because now you know. I wish I would have created or thought of this system when I was your age, but I had to go through the pain first.

Now, as an adult, the pain that I used to feel, has changed to disappointment. I'm truly disappointed that adults still allow jealousy, envy, and toxicity to rule their life and interrupt the flow of others' lives. When I go through the RFSS steps now, if I get to the end and my answer for action is to not be involved with that person, I simply just let them go and move on—and that's ok. I don't need extra hassle in life. I have too much to do—like write this book for you! You have your entire future to do amazing things and this *Red Flag Superpower System* will support you along the way.

Dear Red Flag Superpower Youth,

We are all born for greatness. We are all born full of unconditional love and goodness, and then life changes us. It's inevitable. But how we treat others and expect to be treated is important. We want great experiences in our relationships. The Red Flag Superpower System allows us to narrow our acceptance rate for a more valued relationship experience. This doesn't mean that you can't "work" with someone who you choose to distance yourself from; it just means you will not allow them to deeply affect your life or be in your inner circle. Now that you have this superpower secret, go make the most of your relationships and experiences. Be the person you were born to be—full of potential, goodness and greatness.

You got this,

Mrs. D.

7

COMMUNICATION COURAGE

Communication. It's one of the easiest things to do as humans, and also one of the hardest things. Adults can't even get this right, as I am sure you have experienced in your journey so far. In my adolescent years, I did not communicate well with anyone. Believe it or not, I kept most thoughts in. I became a writer through my silence.

As I went through college, I started communicating better and asking humans around me a lot of questions. I've listened intently for most of my life. I've studied humans for longer than you've been alive. What I've learned is that listening is one of the greatest forms of communication. Listening allows us to obtain more knowledge than talking could ever give us. Think about that! While you are talking, the communication is going outward, but when the communication is entering your being with information, it's our greatest source of knowledge.

But, enough about me, back to you! You can do better than the adults in the world who seem to lack communication skills. You get to see front and center through all of the media sources, just how harsh communication has become. Whether in politics or on Instagram, adults are not showing up as great role models. You can do better.

We all know that even in the best relationships, communication can seem impossible at times. Humans have complicated brains, emotions, motivations, hormones, and beliefs. It's a miracle we can communicate properly at all. Still, communication is one of the most important skills to get right. Communication is the gateway to getting what you want in life, and the deepest connector to other humans. Any time we are able to communicate well, our relationships and life are healthier.

But communication is a skill. A skill is something you work on and learn. We are not born with communication skills. We learn how to communicate through life experiences and watching our parents/guardians and role models around us. We learn from the cashier at the store and voices on social media by how we feel while we listen and watch them. Everyone communicates in different ways and if we pay attention, we can pick up on how to do it well.

How we communicate is how we are seen. How we are seen often determines our opportunities. Can you get a job with how you communicate? Can you lose a job because of how you communicate? Yes.

Let's look at a simple scenario that can happen in high school: you are a good student and have consistently done your work well in school; a bad week comes along where every assignment is due at once; everything outside of school goes wrong too; you can't sleep and you cram to make good grades; you aren't ready for your big history test as a result of your rough week; this grade has the potential to bring your overall grade average down to a C if you don't do well; you take the test even though you are not prepared and you fail it. (This is a perfect example of practicing failure, by the way.)

After you turn in the test you get so upset and fight your tears. You know you could have passed that test if you hadn't had other assignments or had gotten a good night's sleep. You might start thinking negatively about your capabilities and doubt your self-worth. Later in this book, we talk about how grades aren't everything and certainly not a reason to doubt your capabilities or yourself. But for now, in this situation, what do you do to help yourself?

One guess …

You got it …

Communicate.

Be bold and find a moment when you can talk to your teacher. Teachers are not as scary as they appear. If you feel like you let teachers down when you fail an exam, please don't put that pressure on yourself. You have not let anyone down, except for yourself. So, go to her/him and ask if it's a good time to talk. If it is, share your experience and see what you can do to make your grade better. Better yet, communicate *before* the test and let the teacher know what is going on in your life. When you communicate this information, you advocate for yourself. Most teachers cannot deny a well-mannered student skilled in communicating their academic needs.

If the teacher says to come back at another time, then set a better time and show up! Showing up communicates your responsibility in making your academics better. If you don't show up, that also communicates to the teacher that this grade is not important to you, and he/she will not waste their time. Following through is one of the best forms of communication to those around you, no matter the situation. Following through allows people to know they can trust you.

Communication is also nonverbal cues like body language and facial expressions. I lose most of my patience for a student who gives an eye roll. Have self-control and respect for those around you by utilizing attentive body language and facial expressions. Nonverbal communication will take you far!

Here are some simple ways to communicate well with your teachers, principals, coaches, and anyone else to move your life forward. This includes family. These are not in any particular order of importance, and you can add on to this list.

- **Listen.** You will learn a lot.
- **Make eye contact.** Your eyes tell your story. Let people see you.
- **Have positive body language and facial expressions.** Show that you care.
- **Focus.** Focusing on whatever setting you are in defines other's perceptions of you. Everyone's focus looks different, and is easier for some than others, but good teachers and coaches know if you are trying.
- **Written communication.** Writing down your truth is a win when things are hard to say.

- **Follow through.** It's hard to deny anyone their needs when you have consistent follow-through.
- **Hold doors for others.** Such an easy and beautiful form of communication.
- **Be prepared.** Showing up prepared is a great nonverbal communication because it shows your respect and value for the situation/environment in which you are prepared.
- **Be mindful.** There are many perspectives besides yours so make sure you are thinking in every direction before, during, and after communicating.
- **Say "good morning," "have a great day," "how are you?", etc.** All humans notice these communications (especially teachers and leaders in your school).
- **Say "I'm sorry"** when you are wrong and it's needed, but not for everything.
- **Say "thank you"** as much as you possibly can. Gratitude can change any situation.

Dear Thoughtful Youth,

No one communicates like you. Make the most of your own skills to better your life. Grow your skills, be brave and advocate for yourself mindfully. It will enhance your life more than you know.

You got this,

Mrs. D.

8

LIFE LESSONS VS. INTELLIGENCE

Well, isn't this quite the battle? Life lessons versus intelligence. Are life lessons more important than intelligence? I ask this question to my students each year. The answers vary, but a class of seniors who had been through Covid were more vocal about this question than any senior class pre-Covid. They endured a tough time and were graduating unsure if they had the proper education to move forward. They knew they had the grades. They knew they could get into college. They knew that they gave it their all, but they missed a lot of education in that time—like most students in the world.

When I asked them which is more important—life lessons or intelligence—they were sure that, at this point in life, their most memorable growth moments were the life lessons. They honored their intelligence, but felt it wasn't the sole component that would move them forward. They wished that they would have had more life experiences, and less time focused on the GPA.

The truth is, intelligence is not always connected to GPA. Performance mixed with intelligence is directly attached to GPA, but intelligence alone won't get you a high GPA. As we have shared in other parts of the book, grades are important, and you should set out to achieve your goals, but those life lessons … that's a true growth area.

Intelligence comes in many forms, growing alongside life lessons. Have you ever heard about emotional intelligence? Emotional intelligence is not an IQ. But it can take anyone as far as they want to go in this world and it has nothing to do with GPA. How do we gain emotional intelligence? From our life lessons and experiences. Emotional intelligence is how we react, adapt, interpret, control, evaluate, and perceive life events. In fact, some studies suggest emotional intelligence is more important than our actual IQ. How do you react to life? How does emotional intelligence support your endeavors in education?

I am not suggesting that your intelligence alone is not important. This chapter is merely a topic to consider on your journey. There are life lessons that will come your way unexpectedly. During Covid, everyone had to accept that most things in life changed. The life lesson for all of us was to learn how to be more flexible. Life experiences and lessons always shift us into a different state of thinking, reacting, adapting, and living. Our intelligence and emotional intelligence will grow alongside life lessons. So, there's no real winner here between life lessons and intelligence. The win comes from finding a balance between the two.

Dear Intelligent Youth,

Cherish your intelligence and embrace your life lessons. Sometimes these life lessons are really hard to accept, but remember they are there to serve your future. Never take your intelligence for granted and know that the diverse intelligences among us is the beauty of our human race.

You got this,

Mrs. D.

9

GRADES ARE NOT EVERYTHING

Truth is, I'm writing this section of the book after I just completed Psychology semester exams for my students. While we were reviewing, I watched the humans in front of me become stressed. Not only because of the test I was giving, but because of *all* the tests coming their way. This is typical in any school you attend during exam seasons, and there is no doubt that the workload is heavy. But no one in history has navigated the educational stressors and expectations students have today. So, I have empathy for the students sitting in front of me, while also preparing them with high expectations.

I check in weekly with my students to check on their educational well-being. They always enjoy these check-ins because it allows us to problem solve and get it all out so we can move on. When students start saying "I'm stressed," I always ask, "Why?" Eight out of ten times, students respond with, "grades" or "school work." This amount of stress adds up. Every week, you are pushed to the max about grades. You are in a constant state of panic over the pressure you feel around assignments. Grades are the priority in your mind and body—especially in high school because you are preparing for college or a career. However, we know that grades are not the only stressor in your life. We know other factors contribute to how we perform in life. "Grades" just happens to be the biggest culprit for you in the immediate.

When I ask my senior classes, "What is something you wished you knew along your journey before becoming a senior?" Many seniors have said they wished they wouldn't have spent so much time and sleepless nights worried about grades—that grades do not define one's identity. That's pretty insightful.

Don't misunderstand my intention here. Grades are extremely important; they are the avenue to your future right now. But these students are right. They are not everything, and grades—good or bad—are not who you are. You should certainly do your best, but life sometimes takes over and perfection is not real. We are imperfect humans, trying to do our best. When our best is not good enough and life takes over, please know that everything can be fixed with strategies I've talked about with you in this book.

The most important factor in moving through your academic journey is to be your #1 advocate. No matter what you think a teacher thinks of you, we as teachers are morally committed to supporting your success. Teachers will be open-minded if you trip and fall and make mistakes. The only time a teacher feels like their hands are tied and they can't help, is when the student has given up, doesn't show up, doesn't try, or does not want help. If you fit into this category, it's hard for anyone to help you.

I want to share a personal story concerning grades that might resonate with you in your own life.

Around 10:00 one night in my own home, when everyone was finally settled in bed, my daughter called us into her room. We entered and she was crying.

"What's wrong?"

"I have a bad grade in English."

"How do you know?" we asked.

"Because I just checked and there are zeros in the grade book that brought my grade down."

As teacher-parents we knew something wasn't right, and the teacher probably made a human error, or put something that automatically calculated the data wrong.

"I just feel so stupid," she cried.

"Ok … first of all, why are you looking at your grades at 10:00 at night? Second, this is probably a mistake so you shouldn't be feeling less intelligent because of a dip in a grade. This can be fixed."

Needless to say, that conversation took a minute to settle. We explained that tomorrow is a new day and she had to be her own advocate with the teacher in order to get things right. Teachers are human. Teachers make mistakes. Go talk to them for correction or to see what you can do to help the situation. Teachers will never know unless you go to them, and they appreciate these approaches.

I share this story not to embarrass my strong and smart daughter. I share because I know that others go through this same exact scenario whether the grades are an accident or real. Either way, you are your best advocate in getting these situations straightened out.

College may not be for you. I want to make sure that we talk about that here in this chapter. In our education system, we have done an injustice by corralling all youth toward a college degree. Again, I do believe that education is *the* most important tool we can obtain, but who decides what type of education is best? There are all sorts of degrees, certifications, and trainings out there that may not require you to dedicate your next six years. Education is education, no matter where or how we get it. In every country, we need service workers. We need air conditioner and electrical technicians. We need plumbers and concrete workers. We need mechanics and linemen. Our society operates on these jobs. It's up to you to decide what is next. Whether it's a university, community college, travel or trade school—find the best plan for you. One size does not fit all when it comes to education.

Your grades are very important, but they are not everything. Your GPA will help carry you toward what you want in your future, but it is not everything. Here are some simple truths to think about while you go through this educational journey in high school.

- Think about and organize your goals so you know what you expect of yourself.
- Having a balanced and stable emotional state is more important than constantly worrying about grades.

- Having a great work ethic creates a part of your identity and sets you on your path to success naturally.
- Settling your nervous system is the most important health decision you can make for yourself.
- Staying ahead of the game and not procrastinating is one big game changer in not stressing over what is due.
- Utilizing your executive functioning and communication skills will keep you on track.
- Your identity is created by your heart, your work ethic, emotional, and academic intelligence.
- You are a smart, capable, and brave young person, and no one can take that away from you.

Dear Capable Youth,

You are not less intelligent because of the numbers and letters that show up on your grade portal. This is a moment to cry if you need, but not for long, because you have work to do. You have things to fix and make better. Dig deep and find your true identity within your heart, strength, and grit. The rest will work out.

You got this,

Mrs. D.

10

Messing Up = How We Recover

We *all* mess up. Sometimes, we mess up a lot. But let me start this chapter by letting you know that *you are not messing up. You are growing up.*

When I surveyed a group of high school students on lessons they have learned while in high school, they shared that they made a lot of mistakes and messed up quite a bit. But one student took it even further. He mentioned that the level of "messing up" depends on how well we "recover" from that mess up. Wow! This insightful message from a strong member of our society is something all adults should listen to as well. Since we know that we all make mistakes, *how we recover* is the most important part in making those mistakes.

Many times, shame takes over when we have messed up, and it is hard to do anything when feeling shame. Shame is so powerful that it's hard to think outside of it. But thankfully the same thing can happen when we feel gratitude. I always say, "There is not a single emotion that can coexist with gratitude." So, when we do mess up, recovery starts with changing the shame to thanks—but the recovery doesn't stop there. We also have to change how we do things in order to get a different outcome. You have the power to turn any situation around!

Say you make a mistake and are traumatized by your own faults and humanisms. Shame takes over and you don't know any way out or any path to move forward. You can't get out of bed. You beat yourself up and self-forgiveness is nowhere in sight. You allow anxieties and insecurities to creep in. Well, we have all been here. Because we are human and making mistakes never ends. It's kind of exhausting to think about. But because we are human, and tomorrow is a new day, we can start over if we can start the day with gratitude.

In our home, I have a sign hanging on the wall that reads, "Every Day is a Second Chance." I put it in our kitchen so that everyone in my household can read it each morning. Just a little reminder that how we recover depends on forgiving ourselves and others, feeling gratitude for the "mess up" so that we can learn how to do things differently the next time around.

We can feel grateful for our mistakes, because like I've shared throughout this book, growth does not happen without pain, mistakes, and mess ups.

"I am grateful he/she/they broke up with me. I wasn't myself with them. Now I can do my own thing."

"I am grateful I got that traffic ticket so I self-check more now and don't hurt myself or someone else."

"I am grateful my parents caught me making unhealthy choices, so I don't go further into this hole or threaten my future."

"I am grateful my sister/brother was honest with me even though it hurt."

"I am grateful my so called 'friend' talked behind my back, because now I won't waste time on that relationship."

"I am grateful" supersedes any other emotion and is the winning emotion for human recovery. Trying our best to find the positive as much as possible gets you to places you never expected to go in the recovery process of *messing up.*

Dear Recovering Youth,

You are in charge of your recovery efforts when life gets off track.

You are not a mess up. You are growing up.

Forgive yourself and be grateful for your human mistakes, for that is how you become the person you want to be in the future— not only for yourself, but for those you love and will love.

You got this,

Mrs. D.

11

LEAVE THINGS BETTER

In all my years of teaching, there has been a natural decline in cleanliness. Please, when you hear the word "cleanliness," don't skip this chapter. This conversation is far more than the lesson you learned in sixth grade about wearing deodorant. Although wearing deodorant is of utmost importance and life-changing for those around you, this lesson will create a more mindful you—a you that leads to more respect of others and the environments around you. Focusing on cleanliness is a simple way to make yourself better and more mindfully prepared for the world.

Mindfulness is being aware of our surroundings and adjusting so we make the best decisions for ourselves and others. Practicing mindfulness is one of the secrets to maturing in an intelligent way. Others can see your mindfulness a mile away, and it will open doors for you.

I'm sure you have heard the saying, "What goes around, comes around." This is not just a saying—it's truth. We give off energy, and that energy can be reflected back to us. Think about the days you are in a bad mood. What happens to the people around you when you show up quiet, angry, negative, cranky, or even mean? Those around you will reflect that vibe back to you and, unless they have the patience of a saint, will eventually excuse themselves from your presence.

It goes without saying that we should all be mindful of how we interact with other humans. But in this lesson, we are talking less about you and more about your environments. Each physical space you are in deserves the best from you. This could be your room, your kitchen, your school, your grandma's house, your car, etc. Each of these spaces should look and be better when you leave them than they were when you entered.

What do I mean by "better?" Oh, I am so happy you asked! Let me give you a few scenarios that could assist you.

You are at school, and your teacher gives your history class donuts as a reward. You all dig in, but when class is over and the bell rings, everyone sprints out of the room not thinking twice about the mess left behind for the teacher. Open donut boxes, paper towels everywhere, glaze crumbs all over desks. You look back at the room and feel a temptation to help, a tug at your heart, but you need to move on to your next class. What should you do in this scenario? Go ahead … take your time and think on it.

Right! You go back and start cleaning up the room for your teacher, even if it makes you late to the next class. Make the space look great. Help your teacher who so generously gifted you with donuts. You leave the space better than how it was when you walked in.

Next scenario:

You play sports for your school, and the school gifts you perks by allowing you to use their facilities. Every single day that you leave practice, the team leaves a mess with water bottles, clothes, sunflower seeds, wrappers, pre-wrap, shoes, etc. These things and more are left on the field, in the dugout, or the locker rooms. Guess what? Someone (another human) has to clean that mess up—the mess left by a collective group of student-athletes assuming the mess will be magically cleaned up.

Now, you may be thinking, "It's not my job to clean up. I'm working hard. That's a job for the coaches, parents, or custodian." If you are thinking that, you have a hard road ahead in life. Someone else's job? Really? All of those people mentioned above do *not* have this job. They have other jobs. Coaching, parenting, and cleaning for your school, but not to clean up your mess at a sporting event or practice every day. It's *your* job to clean up *your* things. Leave the space you spend time in better than how you found it. This is part of your character whether you like it or not. Taking on this job of leaving things better than how you found them gives you a new perspective because you nurture respect for your environment. You no longer take it for granted, you have pride in it. Get your teammates on the mission too. If your team can show pride in this collective care-taking way, just imagine what can happen on the field.

The energy is real when you take care of the people and surroundings around you. Some people call it karma. But we don't leave things better than when we found them so we can avoid bad energy, we leave things better than we found them because it's the right thing to do. It feels amazing. Soon enough, this behavior and character will enter into all aspects of your life. You will be walking to class and pick up a piece of paper on the ground and throw it in the trash. You will make sure that the dishes are clean when you leave Grandma's house, or you go out of your way to help someone else who is trying to make your spaces better, like the custodians at school. These are the acts of mindful, kind and mature humans. It is the right and cool thing to do and anything else is simply … rude.

Dear Mindful Youth,

This simple concept of being mindful in "leaving things better than how you found them" is a way to take small action steps to becoming a better human. Do it for yourself and others authentically, and the rewards you will receive in life will be greater than you could imagine.

You got this,

Mrs. D.

12

MANNERS MATTER

Since we talked a little bit in the last chapter about mindfulness, I thought I would dig in a little deeper on the topic of *manners*.

Have you ever played life question games with friends or family? These are questions that come up on the internet if you type in "Teen Conversation Questions." There are also family conversation card games you can buy in this genre. Sometimes, for us, we need these conversation starters because our daughter and son aren't sharing much, and this is a way to get them talking. Other times they may want to talk but not sure where to start, and this is a structured way to do that. These questions often lead to further discussion, and they ultimately end up *loving* the opportunity to express their thoughts, beliefs, and opinions. Then in return, we keep learning about them and they learn about us. It's a win-win!

One day over Christmas Break, we asked one of the questions: "Who is your hero?"

My daughter said, "Probably Mama."

"Why?" we asked.

"Because she taught me how to have manners."

Wow! I was so touched and surprised! My kids fight me and roll their eyes anytime I mention manners. So, hearing this proved to me that teens actually do listen and take things to heart.

Manners matter because you can move forward in life more easily with them. Some say it's superficial, but the truth is, without manners, we lose respect that we might otherwise gain for ourselves and from others. Whether you are at school, a place of work, a position on a team or club, without manners, we can lose respect from others before we even have a chance to prove ourselves. Manners are our first introduction to others and part of the legacy you leave behind. When you leave your high school, what are the adults saying about you? "Oh, he was the nicest boy and so polite." That's your legacy. Are manners everything? No. But, they can sure put you in the front of the pack quicker than anything else can.

Cambridge Dictionary describes "manners" as: "polite ways of treating other people and behaving in public; ways of behaving toward people, ways that are socially correct and show respect for their comfort and their feelings."[5]

It goes even deeper than this standard definition. Manners seem to be *for* others, but they reward us. Before someone knows your intelligence, your skills, your talents, or your gifts, they see your manners. Manners are defined not only around eating habits, but so much more. Just like in our chapter about communication, good manners will take you far. Are we respectful with our tone, body language, and expression? Are you looking people in the eyes and being intentional about connection while you are communicating? Are you really listening? Saying, "I'm sorry," and, "Thank you"? Are you holding doors for others when you get an opportunity? Shaking hands? I taught both of my kids when they were very young how to shake hands with intention and look the person in the eyes. To this day, others make positive comments about their handshake because they are surprised at their intention at such a young age—they notice that it's rare. Humans will notice and remember that you walked up, shook their hand, or asked them how they were doing. The reward for your effort is how they treat you in return or what promotions/opportunities you get because they know you as this person who shows up with manners. By the nature of human reflection, little disrespect will happen toward you if you have consistent respect for others.

Somehow over time, replying with a "no" became part of bad manners, when it is not. My students in the past have said that they "feel bad" about saying "no" to adults and peers, because they don't want to be disrespectful, or feel like they are letting them down. They also have expressed that they are somewhat trained to not say "no", that parents who practice respect do not allow "no" as a response because it is disrespectful to elders. Ummmmmm ... let's clear this up quickly. Yes, I'm even guilty of telling my own kids, "Don't say *no* to your mother," until I learned what this conditioning was doing as they became older. I don't want them to appease every situation by saying "yes". That can be dangerous. Can you say, "No, thank you"? Ofcourse, there's always a more well-mannered way to communicate dislikes and denials. But sometimes no means no and it's important to say.

As far as manners go with eating, well, this should be self-explanatory. Someone who sits with their boss over lunch with poor table manners will be less likely to earn that promotion over someone who eats slowly, doesn't smack, wipes their mouth with a napkin, doesn't talk with their mouth full, or slurp their drink. You know what I'm talking about … so be mindful of how manners while eating can impact how you are viewed as well.

Dear Mannered Youth,

This is important! I want to make sure you read the part in this chapter about saying no. I want to make sure you don't think good manners means being run over by humans. Having manners does not mean you say yes to appease everyone. The truth is, some people who are mean don't deserve a lot of respect or yeses. However, that does not mean we treat them poorly. It means you just don't have them in your life, because you have important boundaries. Boundaries are manners and kindness to yourself. Now, go win some people over on your journey by having your best game on with manners.

You got this,

Mrs. D.

13

RESPECT YOURSELF FIRST

Speaking of boundaries and respect. When I was growing up, respecting everyone else was how we showed our politeness and manners.

Our parents told us to:

Say, "Thank you."

Say, "You're welcome."

Say, "Please," and, "Sorry," and, "Excuse me," and, "Bless you," and … Geez, politeness overload!

Guess what? I've taught my own kids to do the same. It's not wrong, but now I know, there's simply much more to the dialogue on respect.

We've talked about skilled communication in a previous chapter. Politeness would fall under the communication and manners categories. These courtesies are great social communication skills for others, but what if we said these things to ourselves? What if every single morning we woke up, looked in the mirror, and said, "Thank you," "I'm really sorry," "You're welcome," "Bless you." Can you imagine how our world would be if we communicated this way to ourselves first? I'm fired up just thinking about it!

If you can respect yourself first, you will naturally protect yourself. Respecting yourself means you know how to be kind to yourself. We know that humans can be mean. Having self-respect first, then sharing that respect with others, is your best protection. Others' pettiness cannot hurt you as badly if you have self-respect. In fact, you won't knowingly let someone hurt you if your love starts with self-love. How? Because when you know your own value, no one can tear it down. You know what you deserve, and you don't settle. Self-confidence is born from self-respect. That's a powerful combo! You can stand tall in your truth of self.

Creating healthy boundaries for yourself is one of the greatest forms of self-respect. When we set boundaries for ourselves, we are essentially setting limits to keep ourselves protected. We also must set boundaries for ourselves. We can easily hurt ourselves by not setting healthy limits in our own actions and emotions. Boundaries are set for yourself, and for others so that everyone knows your limits. When these boundaries are understood clearly, we are being pro-active in limiting unhealthy experiences. We do have to live and learn in order to know what boundaries to set, and when we talk about boundaries, it's worth mentioning that we also need to create balance between boundaries, and experiencing life. This balance can be difficult to figure out, but as you move through life, you will get there.

With self-respect on your side, you will also naturally self-reflect. You will be able to make your own judgment about yourself and change anything that needs adjusting in life.

Self-respect leads to healthy self-reflection and allows us to be the best humans for those we love the most. We become better friends, better students, better everything … because we are better to ourselves.

Dear Respected Youth,

Since our kids were little, we've given them power to have self-respect, and permission to do these three things when someone tries to break their self-respect:

1. Put your shoulders back.

2. Look the person/persons straight in the eye.

3. Tell them to "back off!"

Even if you do these three things in your mind, it works and it works no matter how old you get.

You got this,

Mrs. D.

14

NOT ALL RAINBOWS & BUTTERFLIES

My title here says it all. But, let me expand a little more. Do we wish that life was all butterflies and rainbows, gummy bears and Pringles? Yes! Of course, that's what we want in our lives. We want every piece of goodness life has to offer. We want the least amount of struggle in life possible. But to be perfectly honest, I have never met a single person who said their adolescent years were struggle-free. Not even my own two children.

Although life is never perfect, I have met people who have had a solid and happy teenage experience. As I look back on those who have shared their happy years, I've made a few conclusions. For one, these types of people are rare. Second, these unique teens have a certain mindset for their life to be happy. It's not that they are automatically happy or that life has not been hard on them. Most of the teens who have shared their healthy experience have had tough times and harsh struggles. So, how can they say it's been a good experience?

Well, my dear youth, these teens *choose* to have a good experience. They choose to turn the bad into something growth-worthy and life-changing. They choose to keep waking up and do their best. They choose to take care of themselves and break cycles. They may not always *be* happy, but they are *practicing* how to be happy. We can practice happiness in life when we have minimal struggles. Then … because we have practiced happiness, when things get harder, we don't have to work so hard at convincing ourselves to be happy.

Yes, I can hear you now in my head: "But, Mrs. D., this is impossible. This doesn't work. It's not a Disney story."

Oh, but isn't it? Why do you think Disney stories and others like them are so popular? These stories are written about characters who live through hard times … and make it. These stories are relatable to us. But the characters don't only "make it." They are happy in the end. Now, I will give you this, maybe they are not choosing or practicing being happy. There's not a lot of time for that in the scripts, but the stories remind us that we have something to fight for. It's not all butterflies and rainbows, but the characters still turn their struggles into something beautiful, just like the teens I mentioned above.

You get to choose to work hard for your happy moments. You get to practice happiness. You *get to* create your happy ending. Whenever you think you have no control over anything in your teen years, remember this chapter. Practicing happiness might be one of the most important choices you get to make for yourself during this time.

Dear Happy Youth,

My point to you in this chapter is this: you have so much to look forward to in your life. You get to choose your reaction to life's struggles. I have an important question for you.

When the hard times fade, because they will if you choose happiness, have you practiced happiness enough to really enjoy life? I hope so.

You got this,

Mrs. D.

15

YOU GET WHAT YOU GIVE

We were all born as good humans. We were all born with zero hate, jealousy, or greed in our hearts. There is not a single human born with an intent to hurt someone else. When it appears that humans are bad, it's because life hurt them enough to make them retaliate. *You* were born good, and *you* are still good. This lesson is life-changing. This lesson is not talked about with your age group, and you can thank me later for the practice of "you get what you give." This concept can help you change your own cycles, change other's lives, and make this world better.

Some of you may already *get* the concept of "you get what you give" because someone around you talked about it, and some of you will not learn this until much later in life. But here's an opportunity to learn it now. The reason it's sometimes hard for teens to grasp the concept of "you get what you give" is because you are in the "here and now" of life, thinking of your own needs and rarely reflecting on others or life around you. Not in a bad way, it is the stage you are in.

We have talked about every single move you make right now is a choice. When I say, "you get what you give," I'm talking about your "giving investment." An investment means you may or may not get an immediate return. But the daily work of investing pays off in the long run. I'm talking about the small things that make the most positive impact on our lives. When we give in the simplest and most authentic ways, we will receive that same type of energy in return.

One day, I was talking to a fellow teacher who initiated open classroom discussions to get a good gauge on what was happening with her students. She mentioned that some complaining started, and the students started throwing out names of their peers. Being an emotionally intelligent teacher, she stopped the complaining immediately, and let the class know that there would be no discussion about people who were not present in the room. She continued to remind them that they would never want for someone else to be talking about them. She is right! By talking about others behind their back or in public spaces where the person is not present will bring that same energy back to you. If you talk behind others' backs, *you alone* can create your own social disaster by acting against other humans who do not deserve it. Others will talk behind your back, and no one will trust you in the long run. In other words, *you get what you give!*

A way to keep your life peaceful and in good reputation would be to not talk about others negatively at all. Oh, you're saying that's not possible?

Yes. It. Is.

Of course, it is human nature to have issues with other humans, or them with you. This will happen no matter how old you get. But you can control the amount of drama your life has by being good to others—being true to others and not speaking negatively about them. If you can let others live their lives without talking bad about them, you have won! This sort of giving investment brings you a return of a good reputation, a good feeling in your own heart, and you will be treated with value and respect because you treat other humans with value and respect. I personally know teens who choose this route in life. They let everyone live their lives and stay out of drama. If this is the person you are, who can say anything about you? And if they do, it's actually a reflection of themselves.

Of course, as we have learned, you have to respect yourself first in order to give it to others. A huge red flag moment is when someone is just mean and hurts the people around them. That usually means something tough is going on in that person's life, and/or they have little respect for themselves. You can utilize the Red Flag Superpower System (RFSS) in these instances. Still, give grace until you know your truth.

STOP: *Take a Breather.*

EVALUATE: *Find the Truth.*

CONCLUDE: *Own the Truth.*

ACT: *Proceed or Change.*

Ladies, I hate to call you out here, but the mean girl cliques are one of the worst forms of energy for any environment. The amount of gossip and toxicity that is brought into the world in these groups is deadly. Literally. If someone is talking about others behind their backs in your group, do not trust them! Anyone who can talk about others behind their backs in a negative way, is also talking about you—their "friend"—behind your back. It never, ever stops with one person. Be smart, get out of these mean cliques, and invest your energy in the way that benefits you and the world.

Gentlemen, the jokes that you think are funny at your "friend's" expense are not so kind in most instances. They actually hurt. Be mindful of the "making fun" of others in order to make people laugh. Being funny is different than using someone else as your comedy. This is actually a reflection of your own insecurities. Truly funny individuals don't need to rake humans over the coals to make other people laugh. Invest in being funny on your own and supporting your friends so they can trust you. Be respectful with your words and actions with all people. Then you will see your own insecurities fade away.

"You get what you give" does not only apply to how we treat others. This concept applies to every single thing on our path of life. I've listed some simple ways to give authentically, and in return you will see your own life flourish. Remember, we do not only do these things out of fear of bad things happening. We do them because it's right. These simple actions become habits, and then your heart will do what it was born to do—invest in goodness. Think about the list below and where you are in these action steps. The return investment on these actions is an enriched life.

1. **Be honest**—in all aspects of life.

2. **Be respectful**—to yourself and others.

3. **Be consistent**—so people know what to expect.

4. ***Be the motivator and supporter***—lifting up others around you.

5. ***Be safe***—in all areas of your life.

6. ***Be positive***—it's contagious.

7. ***Be willing to talk about the tough things in life***—in appropriate ways.

8. ***Be trustworthy***—that's what people deserve.

9. ***Be fun***—in appropriate ways.

10. ***Be giving***—with appropriate boundaries.

Dear Giving Youth,

It took me a while to figure this lesson out. I have made many mistakes to get here. I've always been an investor in giving and my returns have paid off even through some poor choices. Save yourself some time and start investing early in life. There's no way to be perfect in this … it's about your intention to do your best in giving and good things will follow.

You got this,

Mrs. D.

16

EXPECTATION VS. INTERESTS

I recently asked high school seniors, "What do you wish you would have known before graduation?" One student responded that she wished that she would have been able to understand the expectations placed upon her, and separate those from her true interests and passions. Wow! This is a huge realization for a seventeen-year-old.

She is right. Adults place a lot of heavy expectations upon you, and you have high expectations for yourself. Play this sport, go to this college, don't make a bad grade, eat this way, don't turn out this way or that way. Ugh! It's so much! Mostly, the high expectations are given with good intentions by the adults trying to guide you. But, when my student shared this one simple sentence with me, "I wish I would have paid attention to my interests as much as my expectations," well, it was a wake-up call for me as an adult. (Proof that kids teach adults.)

With the hustle and bustle of life, and the high expectations placed upon high school students in this day and age, I can very much see why you—our youth—are losing yourselves, not realizing your interests, or pushing them to the side out of survival. You're numbing your passions and your interests, because there is little time for them. These are the choices you feel you have to make and of course, as a good student you rise to expectations. But what if you were able to balance the two worlds? I know it is possible because I see it. But it does require some planning, organizing, letting go, and follow-through.

If we do not feed our soul with our interests and passions, we lose touch with ourselves. We lose the spark of life. Can you talk with your parents or guardians about helping you balance? A teacher? I would love for my wake-up call to be your wake-up call while starting your high school adventure. Above I mentioned that balancing your expectations and interests will require some planning, organizing, letting go, and follow-through. Let's do this.

Plan

Write a list of everything that makes your heart smile and what makes you feel more motivated in life.

Organize

Go through that list and circle two interests/passions that mean the most to you. Write out the time, space, and needs required to bring them to life.

Let Go

There might be other things on your calendar and in life that you will need to let go of in order to fit your true interests/passions into your life. It's ok to let go of some things that are not feeding your soul.

Follow Through

Find balance and take action steps and bring these interests into your life, even if it's one interest/passion at a time. You can do this.

Dear Talented Youth,

I'm writing this chapter because I hope it wakes you up to think about your interests, talents, and gifts so you can act on these interests before you are a senior in high school, regretting that you didn't follow your interests. Find ways to rise to expectations and serve your interests so you can have happier moments. We all need your gifts. It's what makes the world a better place for all.

You got this,

Mrs. D.

17

PRACTICE SAFETY

I'm writing this chapter after my fourteen-year-old daughter just went into the movies with a friend—without adult supervision. Of course, I walked them into the theater, and I'm waiting for them in the parking lot. This is a big change for all of us. But it's time. Obviously, parents make their own decisions about when they feel comfortable with their teen having more independence. In this day and age, it's a little scary. But then I think about my day and age (I won't let you know the century), where we had no cell phone to alert anyone. We were on our own if something happened. Dangerous events happened back then just like they do now. The only difference is we have more outlets to share now. I also think all humans are more alert than ever before.

I wish so much that I did not have to write this chapter. I wish that we didn't have to talk about safety so much. Talking about safety can sometimes bring up fear and make us anxious. But understand, talking through this fear can make any situation easier to understand and help you be proactive on safety steps as you enter into more independence. This is good. It's what you've been waiting for, but how can you be safe without feeling anxious?

The answer is simple. *Practice* safety.

Have you heard of Maslow's Hierarchy of Needs? Maslow is a psychologist who created a tiered system based on his theory that we all are motivated by our needs. These needs are dependent on one another for our life to flourish, however, each tier doesn't always exist alone. The lower needs are sometimes called "survival" needs. Maslow says that these survival needs must be met before anyone can progress to the next tiers. I bring up this theory in this chapter because it shows that safety plays one of the most important roles for us to be successful. Safety is a survival tier. After the need for food and shelter on the bottom tier, we need to feel safe in order to live our full potential. I know that you want to get to the tier stage of belonging and self-esteem, but in order to do that, you must feel *safe first*. Take a look at Maslow's Hierarchy of Needs. Identify what needs you feel are secure in your life and which ones might need some work or where you might feel stuck. For all of us, self-actualization is a work in progress so do not feel you should be there right now. In fact, in my years of discussing this chart with teens, the majority typically hover around the belonging stage and that is appropriate for adolescent years.

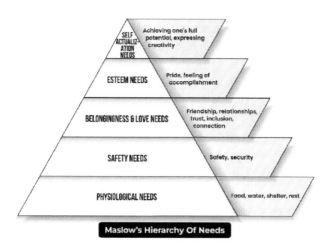

Maslow's Hierarchy Of Needs

Just like the other lessons we are practicing in this book such as, failure or happiness, the more you practice, the more natural it feels. Up to this point, you have had an adult practice safety for you. The adults in your life taught you to cross the street safely, but still had their head on a swivel watching out for you. So, now that you are responsible for your own safety, here are some simple ways to practice it.

- **Be proactive.** Get ahead of any situation that can arise and don't wait for something to happen. The goal is to be "proactive" rather than "reactive."
- **Always stay alert.** Make sure you are looking around and keeping an eye on your environment. I always say, "Keep your head on a swivel."
- **Don't use a noise-cancelling** option on your listening device while you are alone and out and about. This feature prevents you from being aware fully. But by all means use the feature when you are not out and about.
- **Take a self-defense class.**
- **Pay attention** to buildings and spaces you enter, whether the movies, store, or school, always be aware of exit doors and always have an exit strategy.
- **See something–say something.** Probably one of the most important proactive measures. We hear this often, but I'm not sure our youth really take it to heart. If you want to be safe, and for others around you to be safe, we must be brave enough to share important information with those who can help us.

It's *all* of our responsibility to share if we see something unsafe or out of the ordinary. On this topic, it has come to my attention that our youth have a hard time sharing because they don't want to be labeled a "snitch." Wow. Look at how we have allowed our voices to be oppressed. Let me be very clear, snitching is part of our current day safety. The term "snitch" was used back in the 1950s and the safety protocols have progressed since then. But still, kids will hold any secrets to not be called this. Being more scared to be called a snitch rather than calling out danger is some crazy psychology. We are not here to protect those doing wrong. We are here to protect ourselves and others ... period. **The snitch is the hero.**

Dear Brave Youth,

No one should ever ask you to keep a secret if it's bad. Anyone who calls someone a snitch because they told the truth, is a bully. Please, be on the right side of goodness and truth, and be proactive in practicing safety for all.

You are stronger than you even know when you use your truth—and the snitch wins.

You got this,

Mrs. D.

18

Make Good Decisions for Yourself

Well, it's high school. You are going to make a lot of decisions for yourself in the next four years. You will have joint decision-making options with your parents/guardians, and some as a solo decision-maker. Either way, you have the tools to eventually make great decisions for yourself. I've listed three important foundational decision-making strategies that will support all other decisions you will be making. This is where you start. Don't worry, you will make mistakes along the way, you are human.

1. Show Up

You get to make the decision to show up to school, every … single … day. The federal law says you don't have a choice, and you don't, but you do get to choose how you show up each day. Many of my senior students have shared that they wish someone reminded them how important high school was to their future. Some students have even expressed that they wasted learning time because they thought school was a waste of their time. They showed up half-performing or skipped a lot of school because they resented having to go. One person said they wished someone had let them know how important junior year is because they didn't show up and, as a consequence, couldn't get into certain colleges. Listen, I understand, life is hard. There is a lot to juggle. But creating the habit of showing up ready to learn—with your eyes and ears wide open is a gift you can give yourself.

Show up! It's your decision and it directly impacts *you*— no one else.

2. Try Your Best

After you show up, you have the choice to try hard or not. Recently, I was teaching a class with a small sub-group of students who were doing "just enough" to get by. I would give the class the information and assignments, and this small group would complete only half. This small group lacked effort, and their actions affected the entire class's morale. They even started making fun of others who put their *all* into class until I caught on and stopped them. This type of peer pressure shows up many times in school, social, or sports settings. In fact, this will always happen no matter how old you get. People who choose not to give their best, or hate what they are doing, envy those who are giving their best and enjoy what they are doing.

In all environments, there are two groups of humans (there are more group types, but we are talking about two for this lesson). One group wants to bring you down with them through their negativity and lack of trying and knowledge, and the other group wants you to "rise up" with them through their teamwork. You probably already know where you fit in and where you want to be within these groups of humans. Never let someone influence your decision-making to be less than your own greatness. Trying your best doesn't mean you will be perfect. It does not mean you will pass everything with flying colors. Trying your best means you have made a personal decision for *yourself* to put forth the effort it takes to be a better you. What a great decision!

3. Follow Through

Once you "show up" and "try your best," how will you *perform* for your educational experience? How will you follow through? Because when we are talking about "performance," we are talking about complete follow through after you show up and try your best. Listen, Covid times are over for now. There's no more missing school or clubs or practice simply because you don't *feel* like it. The only reason you should be missing anything is if you are bleeding, throwing up, or burning up with a fever. Otherwise, it's your responsibility to follow through with your commitments. We've talked in previous chapters about how following through is a form of nonverbal communication. Making the decision to show up, try your best, and follow through is how you mature and become responsible. It's how you keep getting better at life. You are now someone others can count on and trust. You now love yourself more and can trust yourself more. And … you know what? That anxiety you feel will be less. Many times, our anxiety stems from procrastinating or not following through with promises and commitments we have made to ourselves and others.

Oh, and one more thought on decision-making—let's talk friends. In addition to the three decision-making strategies above, choosing friends is arguably one of the biggest decisions you'll make throughout your high school journey. Your guardians can't help you with this. Friends can make or break your experience in high school and beyond. As the old saying goes, "You are who you hang out with." That is the truth. Making friends is tough. Making best friends who are true to who they are and who you are is just—rare. Proceed wisely.

Dear Good Decision-Making Youth,

There are so many more decisions you will have to make in the years ahead than what I've discussed here. While making those decisions, if you choose to show up, try your best, and follow through, decisions down the road will be easier. Be safe and mindful in your decision-making and know that mistakes happen, and tomorrow is a new day. Oh, and listen up! Don't let anyone take your excitement away—don't let anyone take your best attempts from you—don't let anyone steal your joy in learning new things.

You got this,

Mrs. D.

19

PARENTS OR GUARDIANS (PG)

Believe it or not, parents and guardians (PG) do their best with what they have. I know that's hard to believe when so many things upset you about life right now. In my time working with families, I've seen all sorts of dynamics, and no matter the pain or joy, PGs do their best. It took me a long time to realize this until I could be honest with and understand the fact that adults have a lot of issues and problems too. Adults are human, after all.

I had a student once who was such a polite soul. William was in tenth grade, and he never missed a day of school. Not one. Although he was present every single day, he still struggled in school academically. He had a hard time turning in homework and completing projects. But he was alert while in class. He wanted to do well, and I could see how important school was for him. As we entered into the last days of the school year, I got to know William a little better as a student. Most students don't show up after they have completed their exams. But he did. So, I asked him, "You didn't want to stay home?"

William replied, "It's better for me to come to school than stay home, so I come to school even if I'm sick."

"Why?" I asked.

"Because my parents aren't home very much. They both work two to three jobs and I'm home with my baby sister when we don't have school. We eat breakfast and lunch at school to help my parents financially. My sister doesn't miss school either."

"What part of town do you live in, William?"

"I live in an extended stay hotel off of University so we can come to school here," he mumbled softly.

"Are you and your sister safe?" I asked.

No one has ever looked at me the way he did. He said, "Mrs. D., my parents are good parents. They are working so I can go to college and maybe support our family. I know it's not the best situation we are in, but they are doing their best, and it's ok."

William graduated and went to college on a scholarship. He was filled with pride for his future. His parents were proud. I imagine they knew they had not given William the most proper upbringing and very likely their physiological needs were not met, but look at him now! They did something right, and they did the best they could with what they had.

The key statement from William is "with what they had." I believe anyone can do better, and anyone can break cycles. But some humans do not have the tools or education to change their situation. Humans do what they can—with what they have.

Please don't misunderstand, I do not condone neglectful or abusive home environments in any regard. Anyone in an unsafe situation should find a safe space, seek help, and tell the truth. My point to this lesson is that all families look different—inside and out. William's family was loving and supportive on the inside, but lived a tough life on the outside. Humans are always going through something that no one really knows, so finding perspective is important.

Your challenge is to figure out what you will do with your own experience and life when you're old enough. Will you be the one to break the cycle for yourself and family like William did? Will you be the one who is consciously doing better for your future? No matter if you have perfect parents, there will always be things to change. I, myself, give my own kids open permission to make their lives better than what we could provide. *You* get to make your life whatever you want it to be. But, in the meantime, find a little grace and perspective if you see your PGs doing everything they can to support your life. Adults go through a lot too.

Dear Change-Making Youth,

Just remember, "better" doesn't mean "perfection." I tell my own two children often—your job is to do life better than I have. Even if your PG is close to perfection or having a tough time, breathe through adolescence and give a little grace, say thank you to them when they show up for you, and then, when it's time, go be the adult you dream of in your own future.

You got this,

Mrs. D.

20

THE IN-BETWEEN

We have talked about how frustrating this stage might be for you. Between the ages of thirteen and seventeen, you are still too young to do what you want, but you are too old to be a kid. You feel subtle independence so you want to do more, but you can't do everything you want. You want to be trusted more as you mature, except you're not always making the most mature decisions. You want independence and to take risks, but you miss being that little kid who felt safe and loved no matter what risk you took. You still want those hugs when you make mistakes or get hurt, but that's weird to ask for at your age. The struggle is real. You are all caught in the "in-between." Too young, but too old.

That debit card your parents/guardians gave you at age fourteen so you can use your own money and learn responsibility, well … it has limits and guidelines. That responsibility that your parents/guardians gave you to stay home alone for hours at a time, well … here are the rules and regulations around staying home alone. (And by the way, the house needs to be cleaned and the laundry put away.) Your phone, use it … but not too much! It can all make you want to scream, and you probably do scream. You probably didn't even recognize that all of this is affecting your emotions right now.

Although this stage can be frustrating, you are not alone. It's ok to be sixteen years old and curl up on the couch beside your parents or grandparents when you need them. It's ok to say no to the things you feel you have outgrown. But pay attention to how you communicate all of these changes to those you love the most. Parents and guardians are not always aware of your current stages. Your parents and guardians still see you as their little person who had a free spirit and went full force in life. To see you in your teens as a big person, who has dark emotions and insecurities, well … this change is a tough acceptance. Have you ever watched Disney's "Inside Out"? If you haven't, now is a good time to watch it. If you watched it when you were young, watch it again and see how differently you relate to the movie.

Your parents/guardians love you unconditionally, but these changes are tough on them too. So, if I can help you see their perspective, maybe you can move through these years with more understanding. Maybe even try talking through this chapter with them. You both miss the past, and you don't know how to navigate the unknowns of the now and future. We're all winging it. You also are learning how to love your newness and manage your emotions of missing your younger self. There is common ground in the in-between of the new fabulous you and the beauty of the younger you. You just have to look hard to find it.

Dear New You,

Even while writing this, my heart is emotional thinking of my own kids. I can see their eagerness to grow, at the same time, the confusion and pain of growing up and separating a bit from their parents. For me, I have tried to celebrate every stage and not get caught up in the "missing the past" feelings. Humans are complicated. The only thing we can do is do our best in all stages. All I know is, growth in any form should be celebrated.

You got this,

Mrs. D.

21

DEATH IS FINAL

Don't let this chapter title scare you. This is the most important topic I can possibly talk through with you and we will tread lightly as we move through this chapter.

Chances are, you have already lost someone important, so you already know that *Death is Final.* Before you read this chapter, please be aware that it might be triggering to some, but I am trying to talk about this subject in a different way and give you some action steps.

It would be wrong to not talk about suicide with you in this book. Your age group is one of the most at risk for contemplating the finality of life. As we have talked about in previous chapters, in your middle and late stages of adolescence, many changes occur within your body. But also, changes happening outside of your body that are altering your environments and how humans respond to you. For example, you may feel you've been protected to some degree up to this point by your parents or guardians. You may feel shielded from the real world or from having to make any big decisions. Those closest to you have always kept a good eye on you until now because you are becoming more independent. You want your independence, but you are starting to realize how it feels for some of those protections or securities to start moving further away.

This part of your journey is also hard on your parents/guardians as well. It's all a big shift in life, but the reality is, you might feel like you can't share your emotions or thoughts anymore because you need to keep that boundary of independence. You might feel that you don't want to bother those closest to you with what's going on in your world. You may even feel alone.

This entire part of development is kind of painful and confusing yet liberating. But let's keep in mind that, in the psychology world, these stage changes are called "developmental" stages. According to Merriam-Webster, the definition of "developmental" is: "designed to assist growth or bring about improvement."[6] Wow! You are designed biologically to grow and improve. This is what we mean when we say, "It gets better." You are developing! I get why it's hard to trust the "it gets better" campaigns. You are in the moment you are in, and how can you trust that it gets better? Let me share this again … you are *designed* to get better and improve with time and *that* you can trust. It's not always easy, and it takes a lot of work, but getting through these developmental stages are essential to seeing what your life has in store for you. It's all really exciting when you think about it that way, right?

Ok, so now that we have the basics of our biology understood, let's talk about the momentary impulses of wanting to escape your existence on earth. With all of the life demands and pressures on you, while simultaneously aligning with your natural development and mental/physical health, there may be times where you feel like you need a quick escape from life. Well, it makes sense that a quick escape on a walk, or jog, or drive are ok. But impulsively, you may mean that you want to leave life altogether to escape your feelings. Making the decision to create a permanent escape is not only final for you, but is final for everyone you know as well. Trust me when I say, you are not alone in these feelings. If it's not you who feels this way sometimes, you might have a friend who is contemplating a *final* life decision.

Here's what I have learned over the years from youth: wanting to escape does not mean you want to die and being unhappy is a natural emotion to move through. So, let's talk about healthy escapes for you. We are not back in the 1990s. We are openly talking about suicide now. Someone in your life can help navigate how to help yourself or someone you love who might be thinking of finalizing their life.

In 2021, according to a Youth Risk Behavior Survey, approximately 30% of high school females considered attempting suicide, while 14.3% of males seriously considered suicide. 23.6% of high school females reported having a suicide plan, while 11.6% of high school males made a plan. 13.3% high school females attempted suicide, while 6.6% among high school males attempted suicide.[7]

Let's put that into perspective. If you are sitting in a high school class of twenty peers, research says an average of two to five peers in that class have *thought* about finalizing their life by suicide. One to three peers in that class could consider attempting or actually finalize their life by suicide. You might be one of these statistics sitting in your classes. That's a big wake-up call, right? Do me a favor right now, take a deep breath, feel the air in your lungs and let it out. All right, let's move on.

As a teacher I've known the stats year by year and my heart aches not only for the students who feel desperate enough to finalize their life, but also for the families of these students. This is why I have always tried to teach with as much understanding, love, and guidance as possible, but with boundaries and high expectations. But at the end of the day, my goal is to always instill *hope* within our youth. I also believe strongly that education is the most important tool for keeping everyone mentally and physically well. There is no greater tool in our toolbox than knowledge. Education makes humans think deeper and wider about everything. Education allows humans to gain perspective and understanding. Even in situations of true mental illness, education can help guide our way. Find a teacher or leader you can trust in your school, community, or home for support.

The choice to finalize life is the attempt to escape some sort of pain or pressure for yourself. Although it may end the pain for the person who escaped, much pain is left over in the world and with those you love. What about the people you love the most? You are gone and they will never be the same. Their joy will disappear with you. Their pain will feel unbearable. Think about how you would feel if someone finalized their life, and you were left to try to live a good life. How would you feel?

Death is Final. You do not get second chances to experience your beautiful future. But if you choose to live, there are second chances every single day! If you or someone you know is contemplating finalizing their life, here are some ways to help escape in a healthy manner and become stronger than you ever imagined.

- Call 988 for Suicide and Crisis Lifeline or call 911 if you or someone you know needs support.
- When in trouble, get to the next safe stage until you can get help or think more clearly. This is *everything*.
- It gets better. You are designed biologically to grow and improve.
- Every single day is a new day to do things differently.
- Make a list of all the reasons to continue living.
- Find someone you trust who can help carry you to the next safe stage.
- Write your thoughts down if they are too hard to say out loud.
- Keep taking steps forward. One step at a time. These steps will get you to the other side of your pain.
- Ask to go to counseling. If you can't within your family, go to a school counselor.
- Understand that what you can't manage right now, you will be able to later with your developing tools.
- It's ok to be unhappy. I want to make clear that during these teen years, you will experience unhappy times and painful moments. This does not always mean something is wrong. This is natural

and healthy. No human can be happy all of the time. Allow yourself to feel it and move through it. Be aware of extended unhappiness and seek professional help when you need it.

- All things can be fixed. If you are behind on tasks at school, or making bad grades, all can be fixed. I would urge you to go to the principal, a teacher you trust, a mentor, or counselor. I will be honest with you—as scary as talking to the principal seems, they can move mountains the quickest for you. Anything outside of school can be fixed as well when you find a safe person to talk with.

- No relationship is worth finalizing your life. The right relationships are always down the road and worth waiting for.

- Go for a walk. Go outside. Exercise. Clear your head as many times as you need.

- Find what you love and do it.

- Look up and around at the people, places, beauty, and pain. The world is big, and any situation can change. You get to make this world yours. Get out of the phone or computer and experience the big world out there. It's waiting for you and it's a better place because you are in it.

Dear Beautiful Youth,

I don't even know you, but I believe in you. I hope that if you ever feel like finalizing your presence on this earth, you think about these pages. I hope you know that no matter your situation, you are not alone. You can and will make it through. Will it be a tough road? Maybe. But take it from someone who had to make it through a couple of unbelievably tough roads, your greatness will shine. Your love will win. Your life will make sense.

You really do have all it takes to live a full and happy life. I can't wait to see what you do in your future! We need you here!

You got this,

Mrs. D.

22

PRACTICAL THINGS TO LEARN HOW TO DO WHILE IN HIGH SCHOOL

Check these boxes off as you move through them (not in any specific order). If you do not have someone to teach you these practical to-dos, YouTube is an excellent resource, as I'm sure you know. Continue to add to the list any other things you want to learn.

- [ ] Learn how to create boundaries for yourself.
- [ ] Learn how to make mistakes gracefully and move on.
- [ ] Forgive yourself.
- [ ] Find time for what inspires you.
- [ ] Start doing chores to help around the house without someone having to ask you. Self-responsibility in contributing to the household is a great way to learn self-worth.
- [ ] Take showers and keep your room clean. A clean room is clarity for the brain.
- [ ] Put the time in to learn how to drive well.
- [ ] Know what to do if you were to get in an accident. Learn about insurance and roadside assistance.
- [ ] Learn how to change a tire by yourself.

- Get some sort of job and volunteer as much as possible.
- Learn how to manage your money in your own bank account.
- Learn how to take your car in for an oil change.
- Learn CPR.
- Learn how to grocery shop with a full list by yourself.
- Learn how to say no with confidence (not when your mom asks you to vacuum!).
- Take a self-defense class.
- Learn a little about taxes and how they work.
- Take care of your health. Eat well and exercise regularly even if it's walking.
- Register to vote when you are eighteen. Your voice is needed for our future.
- Find hobbies outside of sports and school.

Dear Most Amazing Youth,

Thank you for hanging with me for this entire book! Whether you read these lessons all at once or one each day, I hope that you use this book when you need it. I wrote this book because I believe in you, and your value to this world is priceless. If you are having a bad day, come back here, and I bet you will find something in one of the chapters that will help. Remember as you travel this journey … love yourself, forgive yourself, and do what you love. Let go of those who make you feel less than your greatness and keep those who lift you up. Lift others up along the way!

I'm here for you. I see you. Make the most of high school and go make this world better.

Good luck!

You got this,

Mrs. D.

ENDNOTES

[1] "Failure," Merriam-Webster, accessed May 13, 2023,
https://www.merriam-webster.com/dictionary/failure

[2] "Insecurities," Merriam-Webster, accessed May 13, 2023,
https://www.merriam-webster.com/dictionary/ insecurities

[3] "Relationship," Cambridge Dictionary, accessed December 28, 2022,
https://dictionary.cambridge.org/us/dictionary/english/relationship

[4] "Manners," Cambridge Dictionary, accessed January 3, 2023,
https://dictionary.cambridge.org/us/dictionary/english/manners

[5] Myers, D. G., & DeWall, C. N. *Myers' Psychology for the AP* Course,*
Third Edition (Worth Publishers, 2018).

[6] McLeod, S. A. "Maslow's Hierarchy of Needs," accessed July 6, 2023,
https://www.simplypsychology.org/maslow.html (Maslow's Chart
in this book was created by the author on 6/28/23).

[7] Gaylor EM, Krause KH, Welder LE, et al., "Suicidal Thoughts and
Behaviors Among High School Students — Youth Risk Behavior
Survey, United States, 2021," MMWR Suppl 2023, accessed July
6, 2023, www.cdc.gov

ADDITONAL NOTES

A special thank you to friends & family who partnered with me to make this book a reality.

Made in United States
Troutdale, OR
08/04/2024

21784113R00073